REMARKABLE
PEOPLE

Michelle
Obama

by Jennifer Nault

Published by Weigl Publishers Inc.
350 5th Avenue, Suite 3304, PMB 6G
New York, NY 10118-0069

Website: www.weigl.com

Library of Congress Cataloging-in-Publication Data available upon request.
Fax 1-866-44-WEIGL for the attention of the Publishing Records department.

ISBN 978-1-60596-665-6 (hard cover)
ISBN 978-1-60596-666-3 (soft cover)

Printed in China
1 2 3 4 5 6 7 8 9 0 13 12 11 10 09

Editor: Nick Winnick
Design: Terry Paulhus

Photograph Credits

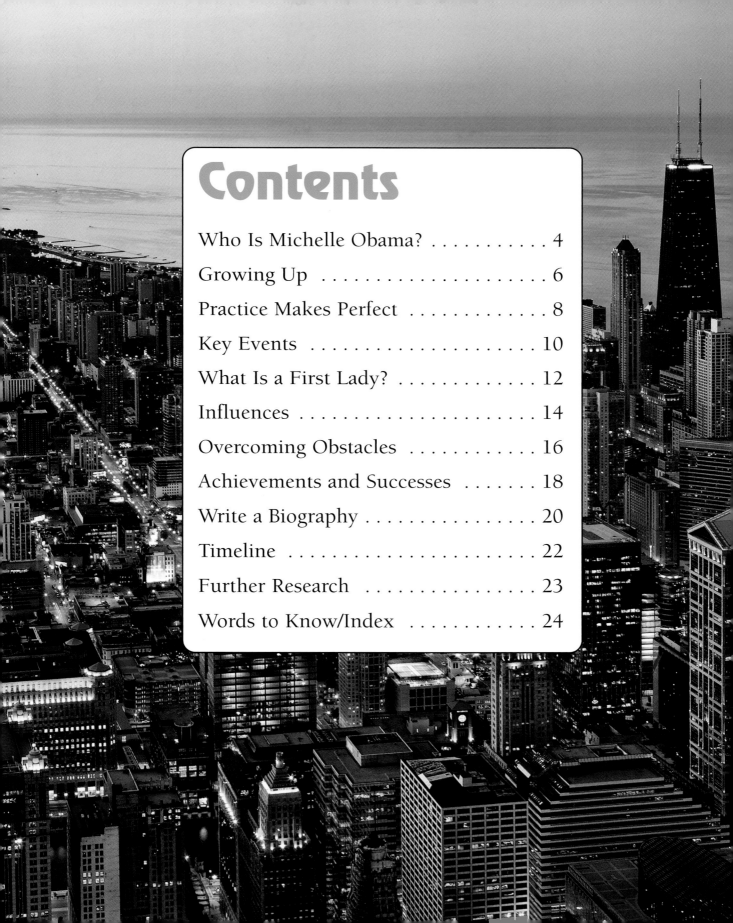

Contents

Who Is Michelle Obama? 4

Growing Up 6

Practice Makes Perfect 8

Key Events 10

What Is a First Lady? 12

Influences 14

Overcoming Obstacles 16

Achievements and Successes 18

Write a Biography 20

Timeline 22

Further Research 23

Words to Know/Index 24

Who Is Michelle Obama?

Michelle Obama is an outstanding lawyer, mother, **public servant**, and **humanitarian**. She burst onto the national stage in 2007 while helping her husband, Barack Obama, **campaign** for the presidency. As the 44th first lady of the United States, Michelle is known for her intelligence, kindness, and style.

Michelle worked hard to gain acceptance into **elite** universities and to become a successful lawyer. She has helped many people through her work in public service, supporting causes that assist low-income families and working with youth in community leadership programs. Michelle played a major role in Barack's presidential campaign, and her efforts were rewarded with his win in 2008. Since the family's move to the White House, Michelle has continued to excite the nation with her bold speeches, humanitarian work, and fashion sense.

> *"I want to help other families get the support they need, not just to survive, but to thrive. They're the causes I carry with me every single day."*

Growing Up

Michelle LaVaughn Robinson Obama was born January 17, 1964, in Chicago, Illinois. Her father, Fraser, worked at Chicago's water plant. Her mother, Marian, stayed home to raise Michelle and her older brother, Craig. Later, Marian worked as a secretary in an office.

The Robinson family lived in a one-bedroom apartment. The children slept in the living room with a sheet dividing their space. Michelle's great-aunt lived downstairs in the same building.

Although they did not have much money, the Robinson family was happy. They liked to read and play games together. Education was important in the household. Michelle and Craig both learned to read when they were four years old.

Michelle grew up in Chicago's South Side.

Get to Know Illinois

ANIMAL
White-tailed deer

FLAG

BIRD
Cardinal

One of the biggest tourist attractions in Chicago is the Museum of Science and Industry.

Chicago is home to the Chicago Water Tower and Pumping Station. This is where Michelle's father worked.

In 1895, Chicago hosted the first automobile race in the United States.

The first skyscraper in the United States was built in Chicago in 1885.

The state motto of Illinois is "State Sovereignty, National Union."

Think about it!

Michelle's family history in the United States dates back to before the Civil War. Since that time, there have been many changes in the way Americans live. Major events and people have shaped the nation. How long have your ancestors lived in the United States? What events have taken place in the country since that time? How has this affected your life today?

Practice Makes Perfect

Michelle's parents knew that education was important for their children. They encouraged their two children to do their best in school and other activities. Michelle was intelligent and loved learning new things. She would work on a subject until she knew it well. When playing piano, Michelle would practice until someone told her to rest.

Michelle skipped Grade 2, and in Grade 6, she was placed in advanced classes. She learned French and studied challenging subjects. Michelle's brother, Craig, was also an excellent student. Michelle would push herself to achieve like Craig.

■ Michelle's brother, Craig, is the head basketball coach of the Oregon State Beavers.

Michelle worked hard in high school. She attended Chicago's first high school for advanced students and made the **honor roll** four years in a row.

In high school, Michelle visited Craig at Princeton College in New Jersey. Craig chose Princeton over other schools on the advice of his father. After visiting Craig, Michelle decided that she would go to Princeton as well.

At Princeton, Michelle focused on sociology and African American studies. She graduated in 1985. Afterward, Michelle went to Harvard, another of the United States' most-respected schools. There, she studied to become a lawyer.

Princeton is one of the most prestigious schools in the United States. Presidents Woodrow Wilson and James Madison also graduated from this university.

Key Events

After graduating from Harvard in 1988, Michelle went to work for the law firm Sidley Austin. She became the **mentor** of a young lawyer named Barack Obama in 1989. He was finishing his law degree from Harvard. Barack asked Michelle on a date, and two years later, they were married on October 18, 1992. Barack and Michelle have two daughters. Malia Ann was born in 1998, and Natasha, or Sasha, was born in 2001.

The young couple worked hard to maintain successful careers and raise their children. Michelle left Sidley Austin to work as an assistant to the mayor of Chicago and as Chicago's Assistant Commissioner for Planning and Development. In 1993, she became the head of the Chicago office of Public Allies. This organization encourages young people to take active roles in their local government. Michelle set fundraising records for Public Allies that lasted more than a decade.

In February 2007, Barack decided to run for the presidential nomination. To support the campaign, Michelle attended events, spoke to the media, and gave speeches about the importance of human rights and education. Barack eventually won the election and became the first African American president.

■ Michelle and Barack, along with their children, Malia and Sasha, became the 44th first family of the United States on January 20, 2009.

Thoughts from Michelle

Michelle has worked hard to succeed in her career and support her family. Here are some of her thoughts about U.S. politics and her life.

As first lady, Michelle enjoys meeting people.

"I love shaking hands. I love hearing stories."

At Princeton, Michelle was surprised by the number of students who came from wealthy families.

"I remember being shocked by college students who drove BMWs. I didn't even know parents who drove BMWs."

Michelle thinks about how her father battled illness while still working.

"We grew up with a father who was on crutches and getting up and going to work every day."

Michelle jokes about Barack's long presidential campaign.

"I might be so tired I don't want to talk to anyone after 2008."

Michelle talks about the state of U.S. politics.

"I think that people are tired. They're tired of the same old kind of politics. People want a new tone to politics. People want to feel hopeful."

Michelle talks about Barack's marriage proposal.

"We were at a restaurant. Then the waiter came over with the dessert and a tray. And there was the ring. I was completely shocked."

What Is a First Lady?

The term "first lady" dates back to the mid-1800s, when James Buchanan was president. Buchanan was unmarried, so his niece, Harriet Lane, would act as his hostess at events. Harriet was referred to as the first lady in an article in *Frank Leslie's Illustrated Newspaper*. The term has been used for the president's spouse or partner ever since.

Though the first lady does not have any formal responsibilities, she plays an important role in the government. The first lady supports the president in his daily activities as leader of the nation. Often, she also promotes important causes, such as literacy or human rights.

The first lady is closely watched by reporters and the public. She is close to the president, so her presence at political events and official functions is important to many people.

■ A first lady can have a great deal of influence and make positive changes in society.

THE WHITE HOUSE
WASHINGTON

First Ladies 101

Martha Washington (1731–1802)

Martha Washington was born and raised on a plantation near Williamsburg. She married her second husband, George Washington, in 1759. Martha was the first woman to become first lady. From 1789 to 1797, Martha served in this role. She was treated as though she were a lady in the British **royal court**. Martha was known to be kind and made visitors feel welcome.

Mary Todd Lincoln (1818–1882)

Mary Todd was the daughter of Kentucky pioneers. At 21 years of age, she met Abraham Lincoln in Springfield, Illinois. They wed in 1842. Abraham was elected president in 1860. As first lady, Mary enjoyed holding social events. However, some people thought she spent too much money. It was the time of the Civil War, and many southerners did not like her **extravagant** behavior. Mary left the White House when President Lincoln was killed in 1865.

Hillary Rodham Clinton (1947–)

Hillary Clinton grew up in Park Ridge, Illinois. She loved sports, as well as school. In 1969, Hillary went to Yale Law School, where she met Bill Clinton. They married in 1975. Both were starting political careers. Bill was elected president in 1992, and Hillary became first lady. In 1993, she chaired the Task Force on National Health Care Reform. This group worked to improve health care for all Americans. Hillary also wrote a best-selling book. As first lady, she supported women's and children's rights. In 2000, Hillary was elected as New York senator, and in 2009, she became the country's secretary of state.

Anna Eleanor Roosevelt (1884–1962)

Eleanor Roosevelt was born in New York City and educated in England. She married Franklin Delano Roosevelt in 1905. In 1933, Eleanor became first lady and moved to the White House. She was a friendly and outgoing hostess who would share her opinions. Eleanor worked to improve the lives of those less fortunate. Following President Roosevelt's death in 1945, she began working with the United Nations.

The President

The president is the first lady's husband or partner. As the president of the United States, his role is to lead the nation. The president is the head of state and head of government. His responsibilities include putting federal laws into effect and acting as the commander-in-chief of the military. This is the nation's highest political position.

Influences

Michelle's parents have always had a strong influence on her life. Her mother, Marian, and her father, Fraser, were role models. Michelle's father had a **disorder** called multiple sclerosis. He was often in pain but always went to work to provide for his family. Fraser never let his illness prevent him from caring for the people he loved. His courage set a good example for Michelle. Fraser also was involved in politics as a Democratic **precinct captain**. Michelle has said that her father's courage inspired her.

Marian taught the Robinson children the importance of education. She encouraged her children to reach for their goals, even if it took a great deal of work.

■ Michelle has always been close with her mother, Marian. Even now, Marian helps Michelle and Barack with their daughters, Sasha and Malia.

Michelle and her brother were very competitive in school. They looked so much alike that they were often thought to be twins. Both Craig and Michelle performed well in school and worked hard to best each other's grades in classes. The hard work and studying skills she built competing with her brother stayed with Michelle as she worked to reach her goals at work and in her family.

THE OBAMA FAMILY

There are four members of the Obama family living in the White House. Michelle, Barack, Malia, and Sasha moved to Washington, DC, in January 2009, when Barack was sworn in as president. Despite the pressures of presidential life, the Obama family remains very close and supportive. Barack and Michelle promised their daughters that they could have a puppy as a reward for making it through the long presidential campaign. In April, Bo Obama, a six-month-old Portuguese water dog became the fifth Obama living at the White House.

◾ The first family enjoys spending time together and walking their dog, Bo.

Overcoming Obstacles

Michelle encountered obstacles early in life. Her parents did not have much money and could not afford special lessons or expensive clothing for their children. They kept a positive attitude and believed that focusing on education could help them improve their lives.

Another challenge the Robinson family faced was **racism**. As a young girl, Michelle learned that her great-great grandfather, Jim Robinson, had been a slave. Slaves were considered the property of their masters and had no rights. They were **discriminated** against because of their cultural background. However, Michelle was born in a time when civil rights were improving for African American people. Even though she still had to deal with racism, Michelle had more opportunities to succeed than African Americans from earlier times.

■ The first African American to graduate from Harvard University was Richard Greener. He graduated in 1870 and became a lawyer and educator.

Later in life, advisors in high school discouraged Michelle from applying to Princeton College. Michelle did not give up her dream and applied to Princeton. She was accepted and was one of a few African American students to study there at that time. Later, Michelle's college counselors advised her not to apply to Harvard. Despite their doubts, she was accepted there as well.

While she was working as a lawyer, Michelle's father died from his long battle with multiple sclerosis. Michelle was deeply saddened and began to think about her father's life and how he had influenced her. She quit her job at the law firm and started working for a non-profit group that trained young adults to work in public service. She helped many people who, like her father, were working to build a better life.

As first lady, Michelle is committed to helping people achieve their goals.

Achievements and Successes

Michelle is a successful businesswoman, first lady, and mother. Memories of her father inspired her to help people by working on social issues. To do this, Michelle has taken important public roles.

In Chicago, Michelle served as the assistant to Chicago mayor Richard M. Daley. In 1993, she helped to create Public Allies Chicago. This organization trains young people for jobs in public service. Three years later, Michelle helped form a student volunteer group at the University of Chicago. Next, she ran the community and external affairs division for University of Chicago Medical Center. She continued working in this job when Barack began his presidential campaign.

Michelle Obama's career is remarkable, yet she believes that her family—especially daughters Sasha and Malia—are her greatest achievements. Even while traveling, giving speeches, and attending events all over the country, Michelle tries not to be away from her daughters for more than one night.

■ Michelle and Barack Obama hosted a party celebrating musician Stevie Wonder.

Since Barack began his run for president, Michelle has become well known across the United States. She has been a great help to her husband as well. Barack says that Michelle keeps him focused.

Michelle is admired for her intelligence, beauty, and her sense of fashion. In May 2006, *Essence* magazine named her one of the "World's Most Inspiring Women." Michelle was chosen among "The Harvard 100," a list of important **alumni** of that school. For her style, *Vanity Fair* and *People* put her on their best-dressed lists.

PUBLIC ALLIES

Michelle directed Public Allies Chicago for almost four years. Public Allies is an organization that helps young people become community leaders. Through the organization, young people learn leadership and organizing skills. They are taught how to influence government decisions on a local level to help improve communities. Public Allies hopes to get communities more involved in the decisions that affect them. **www.publicallies.org**

Write a Biography

A person's life story can be the subject of a book. This kind of book is called a biography. Biographies describe the lives of remarkable people, such as those who have achieved great success or have done important things to help others. These people may be alive today, or they may have lived many years ago. Reading a biography can help you learn more about a remarkable person.

At school, you might be asked to write a biography. First, decide who you want to write about. You can choose a first lady, such as Michelle Obama, or any other person you find interesting. Then, find out if your library has any books about this person. Learn as much as you can about him or her. Write down the key events in this person's life. What was this person's childhood like? What has he or she accomplished? What are his or her goals? What makes this person special or unusual?

A concept web is a useful research tool. Read the questions in the following concept web. Answer the questions in your notebook. Your answers will help you write your biography review.

- What did you learn from the books you read in your research?
- Would you suggest these books to others?
- Was anything missing from these books?

- Where does this individual currently reside?
- Does he or she have a family?

- Where and when was this person born?
- Describe his or her parents, siblings, and friends.
- Did this person grow up in unusual circumstances?

Your Opinion

Adulthood

Childhood

WRITING A BIOGRAPHY

Main Accomplishments

Help and Obstacles

Work and Preparation

- What is this person's life's work?
- Has he or she received awards or recognition for accomplishments?
- How have this person's accomplishments served others?

- What was this person's education?
- What was his or her work experience?
- How does this person work; what is or was the process he or she uses or used?

- Did this individual have a positive attitude?
- Did he or she receive help from others?
- Did this person have a mentor?
- Did this person face any hardships?
- If so, how were the hardships overcome?

Timeline

YEAR	MICHELLE OBAMA	WORLD EVENTS
1964	Michelle Robinson is born on January 17, 1964.	President Lyndon Johnson makes his first State of the Union speech, and declares a "war on poverty."
1985	Michelle graduates from Princeton with a degree in sociology.	Tancredo Neves is elected as the first **civilian** president of Brazil in 21 years.
1988	Michelle receives her degree from Harvard Law School.	The **Soviet** army begins removing its forces from Afghanistan.
1992	Michelle marries Barack Obama.	George H. W. Bush becomes the first U.S. president to address the Australian government.
1993	Michelle becomes the Executive Director of Public Allies Chicago.	Nelson Mandela, president of South Africa, wins the **Nobel Peace Prize.**
2002	Michelle begins working as the community affairs director for the University of Chicago Hospitals.	Switzerland joins the United Nations.
2009	Michelle becomes first lady of the United States.	Secretary of State Hillary Clinton travels to the Middle East to negotiate for the new administration.

Further Research

How can I find out more about Michelle Obama?

Most libraries have computers that connect to a database that contains information on books and articles about different subjects. You can input a key word and find material on the person, place, or thing you want to learn more about. The computer will provide you with a list of books in the library that contain information on the subject you searched for. Nonfiction books are arranged numerically, using their call number. Fiction books are organized alphabetically by the author's last name.

Websites

The Obama's official website is found at
www.barackobama.com/about/michelle_obama

To learn more about Michelle Obama, visit
www.whitehouse.gov/administration/michelle_obama

Words to Know

alumni: graduates from a particular college, such as Harvard

campaign: a political team's plans to win an election

civilian: a person who is not a member of the military

civil rights: the basic rights guaranteed to the citizens of a country

discriminated: treated a person unfairly because of his or her race, gender, age, or physical or mental condition

disorder: an illness causing unusual functioning of the mind or body

elite: special and well respected; sometimes valued for tradition

extravagant: making a big display of overspending

honor roll: being on the top of the list of achievements and grades in school

humanitarian: having care and compassion for good causes; acting in a way to help others in need

literacy: learning and teaching reading

mentor: a wise and trusted teacher

Nobel Peace Prize: an international prize to recognize the person, people, or groups who make an important impact in their fields

precinct captain: an individual who acts as the direct link between a political party and the voters in a community

public servant: a person who works for the government

racism: hatred or intolerance of another race

royal court: the family of a royal leader

Soviet: the former Union of Soviet Socialist Republics

treasurer: person whose role is to oversee the financial matters in a group or organization, performing duties such as bookkeeping

Index

campaign 4, 10, 11, 15, 18

Chicago 6, 7, 9, 10, 18, 22

civil rights 9, 16

Clinton, Hillary Rodham 13, 22

Harvard University 9, 10, 16, 17, 19, 22

lawyer 4, 9, 10, 16, 17

Lincoln, Mary Todd 13

multiple sclerosis 11, 14, 15, 17

Obama, Barack 4, 10, 11, 14, 15, 18, 19, 22

Obama, Malia 10, 14, 15, 18

Obama, Sasha 10, 14, 15, 18

Princeton University 9, 11, 17, 22

Robinson, Craig 6, 8, 9, 15

Robinson, Fraser 6, 14

Robinson, Marian 6, 14

Roosevelt, Anna Eleanor 13

Sidley Austin 10

Washington, Martha 13

White House 4, 13, 15